# Figure Painting

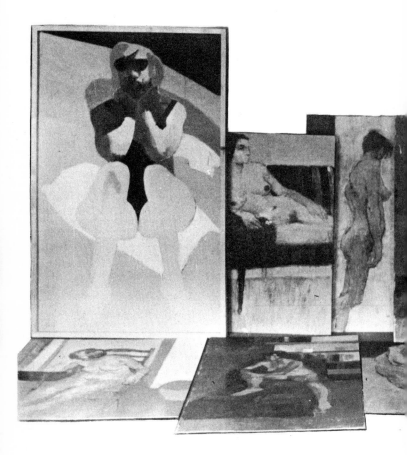

# Figure Painting

## Hans Schwarz

Studio Vista London

Watson-Guptill Publications New York

General Editor Jean Richardson
© Hans Schwarz 1967
Published in London by Studio Vista Limited
Blue Star House, Highgate Hill, London N19
and in New York by Watson-Guptill Publications
165 West 46th Street, New York 10036
Distributed in Canada by General Publishing Co. Ltd
30 Lesmill Road, Don Mills, Toronto, Canada
Library of Congress Catalog Card Number 68–11196
Set in Univers 8 and 9 pt.
by V. Siviter Smith & Co. Ltd, Birmingham
Printed in the Netherlands
by N. V. Grafische Industrie Haarlem

# Contents

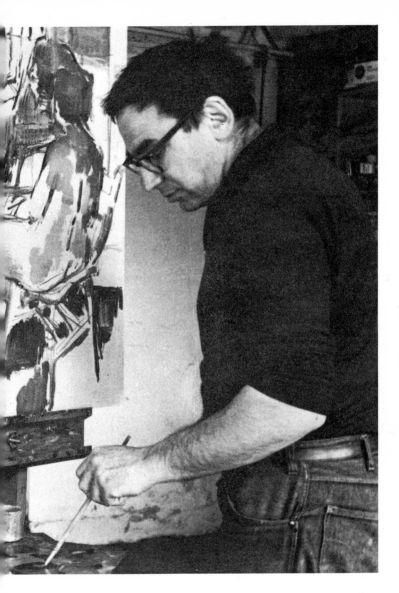

# Introduction

In the 18th century painters were divided into categories. The painter of religious works came first, the most respected. Then came the portrait painter, the landscape painter, the still life painter, and last the animal painter, the humblest—he dined with the servants.

There are divisions today, but they are not by subject. They are aesthetic divisions. Style is the criterion.

To reach their chosen or gradually evolved styles, nearly all painters have undergone the disciplines of art school.

In spite of all new developments, painting from the nude, a tradition reaching back 500 years, still continues and is indeed right at the core of the artist's growth and training. Cézanne, the founder of modern art, aspired to paint ambitious compositions with bathers. The consolidators of modern painting, Matisse and Picasso, are unthinkable without their figure painting. Nearer today still, Kokoschka, Henry Moore, Giacometti, Francis Bacon and Larry Rivers, very much among the *avant garde* of their generations, constantly use the nude in their work.

Why should this rather odd subject, a naked human being, be so important to the artist and so capable of a range of personal interpretations?

We do not see naked people in every-day life. Laws and taboos forbid nakedness in public. Only the more disreputable stage or screen shows it. Educational films about backward tribes are an exception, made permissible by the distasteful implication that the subjects are not really quite human.

But ever since the 15th-century rediscovery of the Greek and Roman mastery of the human body, artists have worked habitually from the nude model. The subtleties of surfaces and colour, the infinite variation of movement, the intricacies of foreshortening and volume are inexhaustible. It is a subject literally close to all of us—we all inhabit a body. This human and (it would be hypocritical to ignore it) the erotic aspect, make it a subject of universal interest. Sculptors have accepted the subject to such an extent that it seems odd to see a piece of sculpture of a fully dressed person—unless he is a statesman or general—on a public monument. Even they have been sculpted in a state of nature.

This acceptance of the nude as a subject has made it possible for artists to find in it the means for experiment. The artist's personality and interpretation, not the model's appearance, have become the real concern.

You can see that I think of figure painting as more than an exercise to improve one's facility in rendering realistic appearances. It certainly does this. Weaknesses are unfailingly exposed. At first the problem of conveying the pose, solidity and movement will tend to put any more ambitious intentions beyond your reach. But, whilst you struggle with basic problems, inevitably something of yourself, your personality, will be reflected in the painting. One never reaches a stage when one can say: now I have learned all there is to learn, now I can begin to experiment and be original. It is a gradual process. Attainment of facility and discovery of one's own personal way of working go hand in hand.

Working from the life model is not the only way to paint figures. Paintings can be based on drawings, photographs or memory. Bathers or workmen, dancers or athletes are related subjects.

I try not to lay down the law too rigidly. But when one feels strongly about a subject it is difficult to be detached and objectively to take note of every possible point of view. If you think that something I say is not for you, ignore it. No worthwhile teacher would wish to impose his way of working or seeing on a pupil whose bent is in a different direction.

Framing, exhibiting or selling are not discussed. My concern here is with painting. If you are a beginner, your paintings will be of more interest to you than anyone else. Spend on paints, rather than frames or submission fees. In any case paintings of the nude are among the least saleable.

The paintings reproduced in various stages in chapters 4 and 5 were painted for this book. The techniques, poses and compositions were chosen to illustrate definite points. Whilst painting them I was pre-occupied with having to recognise a stage when they ought to come off the easel to be photographed. So please take them as teaching diagrams, rather than finished, serious paintings.

# 1 The model

The difficulties of figure painting start before you begin to paint. It can be hard to find models. In large towns there are model agencies which will help, but in small towns or in the country it is not easy.

One solution is to join a class. Local adult education authorities organise evening classes in most areas. You will have to accept whatever pose the instructor sets and you will have to work from it for as long as he decides. But there are many advantages.

The fees are small. You will get instruction. The most indifferent teacher is of more use than the best book (even this one). A teacher can see your mistakes as they occur and guide you according to your needs. A book can only try to anticipate likely problems in a general and impersonal way.

You will see other people's work, which is stimulating. Do not be afraid that you will be too much of a beginner, too unskilled. Teachers prefer beginners who will make progress to people who are set in their way of working.

Many professional artists organise groups or classes in their studios. These are usually somewhat more expensive than local authority classes, but the numbers are smaller and the atmosphere often more congenial. They are advertised in art journals like 'The Artist', 'Arts Review', 'Amateur Artist' and 'American Artist'.

Summer and week-end courses are held, either organised privately or by education authorities. These too are advertised widely.

You probably know people in your neighbourhood who paint. Approach them with the suggestion of forming a life painting and drawing group. It is easier to persuade someone to pose for several artists than just for one. Advertise in the local press or in one of the art journals and you may well have a good response. You share expenses and have a choice of rooms in which to meet. Working in a group will encourage you to go on painting, when on your own you would often get discouraged and feel that to make someone pose for that daub is a bit ridiculous – not only beginners feel that.

If you organise a group, make every member pay their share of expenses (model's fee, heat, light and refreshments) in advance for several sessions. One can lose one's initial enthusiasm; this will help to retain it.

If you are let down by your model—this will happen sooner or later—one of the group can sacrifice himself and sit for a portrait.

Try to meet weekly for a 3-hour session and keep the same pose for two weeks; six hours on one painting is about right. Pay your model the usual fee. Posing is hard work, boring and chilly. He or she deserves a reasonable reward.

Make sure that the room you use as a studio is warm and free from draught. Provide an extra electric heater near the model. It may seem warm to you, but the model is naked and immobile. Provide somewhere for the model to change, another room or at least a screen.

For a painting taking several hours it is worth taking some trouble over finding a pose from which you can work well. Let your model move around and stop him or her when you see a pose you like. Be satisfied with simple, natural poses.

Do not try to arrange your model in poses you have seen in paintings or photos. Everyone is built differently and what looks fine in a Renoir will probably be wrong for your model.

But any model is a good model. Good-looking models are not necessarily the most interesting. As with heads, so with bodies; age can add character. Some models, proud of their looks, will try to pose 'gracefully'; discourage this. Paintings done from such poses look stilted.

Make sure the model is comfortable. Even the simplest pose, held for a long time, causes aches and pins and needles. Allow regular rests—a quarter hour in every hour is customary. Standing poses are very exhausting and may need more frequent rests.

If you use drapery, make sure you can leave it in position for the length of time your painting will take. It can never be re-arranged into the same folds after it has been moved.

As soon as you have decided on a pose, chalk-mark at key points where the model makes contact with floor or chair. This will make it easier to resume the same pose after a rest or at the next session. Also mark the position of your easel.

Do not be too concerned if the model moves slightly—you are after all working from a living being, not a plaster-cast. In most poses a slight relaxing is inevitable. The head will gradually droop a little, the shoulders will sag. The model will not mind being told to move back to the original position, but don't fuss about it; you are interpreting, not copying. I have found in life classes that the worst complainers about the model having moved are the worst painters.

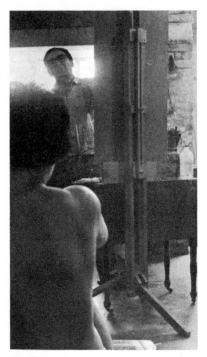

Fig. 1

It is best to look along a straight level, rather than downwards, at the model. A platform or dais is therefore useful, but (particularly if you paint sitting down) not essential.

Keep backgrounds simple: doors, windows, radiators, other artists at work, rather than contrived settings of cushions and velvet drapes. Mirrors are useful. Apart from the compositional interest a mirror adds, it is instructive to see the other side—the hidden arm, how a leg is tucked away.

Use good, strong, flat light—light that will let you see as much as possible and allows you to gather most information, rather than one that gives dramatic, stagey effects. Light on your painting is as important as light on the model.

I paint with my easel about six feet away from the model. If you are nearer you cannot take in the whole figure at a glance. If too far away—over 15 feet—you will not be able to see modelling three-dimensionally, and the figure goes flat. This is my personal feeling; but some artists work at least 20 feet away and they have reasons and arguments to back this up.

You must have room to step back from your painting; do not place the easel so you are working with your back up against a wall. The same applies if you are working sitting down. In fact, the closer you are to your painting, the more often you must look at it from a distance.

Each model presents different problems, having different proportions, colours and ways of moving and posing. Use male, as well as female models. I must apologise for having mainly paintings from women in this book. But I, and many other artists, find it hard to paint from the male model. This is not because it is more difficult, but because the scientific curiosity and interest in anatomy which motivated renaissance painters is long spent. Moreover, male nudes look out of place painted in domestic settings, the only settings available to most of us. Also, and this is the most important point, the shapes of the female body are simpler and more generous. They can be more successfully organised as a painted surface.

# 2 Materials

There are basically two ways of painting: with transparent washes, such as watercolour, or with solid, opaque pigment such as oil paint or gouache (opaque watercolour).

Every painting consists of the *ground* – paper, board, canvas – whatever you paint on, and *pigments,* the colours.

Colours are sold ready-ground and mixed with a binding medium: oil in oil paint, gum in watercolour and gouache (another word for body-colour or poster-paint). A plastic is the binding medium in acrylic and emulsion paints. The Old Masters would gladly have exchanged their secrets for the vast supply of cheap and reliable paints, brushes, canvases and boards we have.

Oil paints can be thinned with turpentine or white spirits (turpentine substitute). Water is used in the other techniques to thin the paint.

Oil paints that have been thinned lose their gloss unless oils, varnishes, gums or plastics are added to the thinning medium.

Paints can be put on by brush, palette knife, fingers, Aerosol, spray-gun, rollers or squeezed straight from the tube.

This book is concerned primarily with oil paint.

## Paints

Please don't buy one of those boxes of paints, containing about 40 tiny tubes of oils, miniature bottles of turps, linseed oil and varnish, a sweet but useless little double dipper, a mini-palette and two-and-a-half anaemic brushes. Even a lack of talent is not as inhibiting as these outfits.

Begin with a restricted number of colours. Every painter works differently and gradually evolves his own palette. This range, which is similar to the one I use, should enable you to mix most colours:

*White.* You will use far more white than any other colour, so get the largest tube possible.

I use mainly 'Mastercote', a semi-prepared Titanium White intended for decorators, but there are other makes on the British market. Thinned with white spirits it forms an undercoat; used with linseed oil or varnish, a gloss paint. But used straight from the tin it has a consistency only slightly thinner than tube colour, but less fatty. Its advantage, apart from cheapness, is the rapid drying which permits effects not possible with artists' white. It dries matt and imparts to oil paint something of the quality of gouache. You may dislike it and prefer artists' colours, but if you find tube paints a bit greasy and slithery, give it a try. There is nothing quite like this available in America, but there are many so-called 'underpainting whites' in tubes, which dry quickly, are less oily than the normal oil whites, and have a slightly matt tone.

*Cadmium Yellow Light.* A sharp, strong yellow.

*Yellow Ochre.* A duller, denser, opaque colour.

*Raw Sienna.* Rather similar to Yellow Ochre, but warmer and much more transparent.

*Light Red.* A fierce terra-cotta red, to be used most sparingly as it has extreme covering power.

*Burnt Sienna.* A more gentle reddish-brown, transparent. It can be used for glazing (transparent layers of colour).

*Cadmium Red.* Strong, cool, bright red—for mixing purples and sharp pinks.

*Burnt Umber.* A warm, deep brown, often used for the initial lay-in or drawing.

*Raw Umber.* A much cooler dark brown, fairly transparent and useful as a neutralising colour.

*Prussian Blue.* Be careful; it is very powerful. But it is versatile as it can be mixed with yellows to make bright greens, and with reds to make purples.

*Viridian Green.* Often mixed with reds, pinks and browns to cool them down.

*Ivory Black.* There is an old prejudice against the use of black, but I see no reason why you should not use it.

Buy your colours in large tubes; it is cheaper. Use them generously. Squeeze out a good dollop of each colour, meanness on the palette is reflected in the painting. Experiment, and use other colours apart from these as you feel the need or temptation.

Paint manufacturers mark artists' colours with the degree of permanence of the pigment. It depends how much you think posterity will value your work whether you avoid the more fugitive colours.

**Ground or support**

Paper, wood, linen, silk, cardboard, asbestos, metal, stone, leather, plastic, glass, linoleum and ivory—anything can be painted on, as long as it is not too rough, is not liable to shrink, stretch or warp and is not too absorbent.

The most usual grounds – paper, wood, canvas and hardboard – are absorbent; so a filler or sealing film (priming) ought to be put on.

The work of the Old Masters has lasted well, but the traditional lengthy preparation of wooden panels with many layers of gesso (plaster) and glue need not concern us here. We don't have a workshop full of assistants and apprentices to do it for us.

Canvas can be bought primed. This is costly, and costlier if it is bought ready stretched. But you can buy raw canvas and prime and stretch it yourself. One coat of glue-size and one of under-coating, or one coat of emulsion paint and one of under-coating, will give a dense, smooth, non-absorbent surface. If, after the first coat, the canvas has rough, hairy bits sticking up, rub it with medium grade sand-paper before putting on the second coat. It can then be either tacked on a stretcher or pinned to a drawing board. On a stretcher the canvas will have a certain 'give' which some painters like.

A canvas-imitating, embossed paper seems to me inferior to good, thick, white drawing paper. This makes a surprisingly good painting ground even without priming.

Old paintings, as long as the canvas is sound and the painting is not too glossily varnished, make a good ground. It can either be painted on as it is or it can first be covered with white under-coating. Under-coated plywood can also be used.

My usual painting ground is hardboard (untempered Masonite). All the paintings of mine in this book were done on it. It is cheap, needs no stretcher or backing, can be cut to any size, is permanent, reasonably light in weight and is easily obtainable.

At a pinch it can be painted on unprimed. But usually I under-coat a whole 4 × 8 ft. sheet of hardboard and saw off a piece the size of the painting I decide to do.

There are painters who use the rough, textured side. At first glance this offers a surface not unlike canvas; but it is far rougher and has an unpleasant, pitted texture which makes fluent work difficult. Several coats of undercoat are needed to fill the deep crevices.

I always use the smooth side. Undercoating, thinned liberally with white spirits and put on freely with a large brush, provides a good painting surface after only 4 to 6 hours drying.

Hardboard can also be made non-absorbent by an application

of glue-size. Add size to hot water—instructions are usually given on the packet—and paint the hardboard with this. You will then have a painting surface of the rather pleasant brown colour of the board. Shellac, thinned with alcohol, is also good. It is, of course, also possible to use coloured undercoating rather than white, if you prefer a coloured surface to work on.

## Brushes

Get used to having several brushes in use at the same time, with some of different shapes and sizes in reserve. Do not start painting with less than six, and be prepared to buy more brushes frequently. Every artist I know has a vast selection, jars and vases full of them.

Mainly hog-hair (bristle) brushes are used for oil painting, but at least one sable brush, which can be an old watercolour brush, is necessary for fine lines.

Begin with a 1 in. and $\frac{1}{2}$ in. flat, a $\frac{1}{2}$ in. and a $\frac{1}{4}$ in. filbert, a $\frac{3}{16}$ in. round, and a pointed, fairly large sable brush, see Fig. 2.

I use decorators' brushes, $\frac{1}{2}$ in., 1 in., and larger too, for big

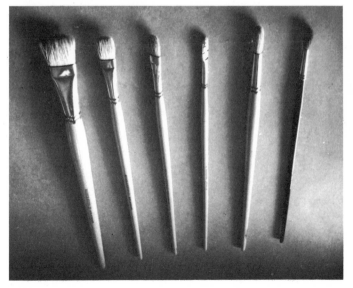

Fig. 2

areas of colour. They are surprisingly adaptable, having much longer bristles than artists' brushes. A good one will do quite delicate work.

Buy good-quality brushes with long bristles or hair. They are more pleasant to use, more flexible and keep their shape and last longer than cheap ones.

Keep your brushes clean. Whilst you are painting, when you have finished with any one colour, wash your brush well in white spirits and wipe it on a rag. When you finish for the day, wash your brushes first in white spirits and then with soap or detergents and water. Work up a lather by stroking the brush backwards and forwards on your palm (Fig. 3). Repeat this several times, rinsing the brush under the tap in between till the lather stays clean, then rinse in clear water again. Stroke it into shape with a dry rag to ensure that the brush retains its shape in drying.

Never leave your brushes in white spirits or water, business-end down, for any length of time. This will distort them and it will be difficult to get them back into shape.

Fig. 3

Make brush washing a not-to-be-put-off routine. Every painter does it; must do it.

For mixing paint, for scraping areas of paint you wish to alter, and for cleaning your palette, a palette knife is essential. There are several kinds available. Get a flat one with a blade about 4 in. long. The type with a bent shaft between handle and blade is known as a painting knife (Fig. 4).

Fig. 4

## Palettes

Any smooth, hard, non-absorbent surface can be used. There seems little reason why one keeps on buying the traditional, shaped, wooden palette. Glass, Formica or enamelled metal-topped tables make excellent ones and are used by many painters. For gouache and acrylic I use an old enamelled fridge top. But (a matter of habit) for oil paint I have a wooden palette. It is shaped with a thumb hole, meant to be held in the left hand while painting; but this is tiring and cumbersome. Use a table to put your palette, paints and brushes on. If, like my table, it has casters, all the better.

Make a habit of squeezing your paints in the same order round the edge of the palette. I start with white at top right and go anti-clockwise through yellows, reds, browns, green, blue and black, leaving the centre for mixing. Keep the colours around the periphery as clean as possible and make sure that there always is a clear area for colour mixing.

Mix even quite small quantities with the palette knife. Mixing with the brush makes paint work its way up the ferrule. Unmixed colours lodge in the brush and make it difficult to clean.

## Medium

White spirits, bought by the pint from a hardware shop, does equally as well at a fraction of the cost as pure turps bought from an art shop. All it has to do is thin the paint and clean your brushes.

19

Fig. 5

It evaporates entirely as the paint dries, doing the job that water does for gouache and watercolour.

For richer, glossier paint, particularly in the later stages of a painting, mix a third to a half linseed oil with the white spirits.

Don't use one of those tiny double-dippers; any jam jar, paint tin, old cup or tumbler serves better. I have a jam jar of white spirits for washing brushes and a large sign writer's clip-on dipper for painting. Being firmly clipped to my palette this cannot upset in use.

### Easels

It is by no means essential to have an easel. Bonnard painted masterpieces on canvas pinned to bedroom walls, and they were walls covered in strident wallpaper.

An easel is useless if it is not firm. A studio easel is ideal, a sturdy radial easel (Fig. 6) is a good second best. Wobbly, so-called sketching easels are useless; far better use a chair to prop your painting on, resting the palette on the seat, and sit on a facing chair, (Fig. 7).

20

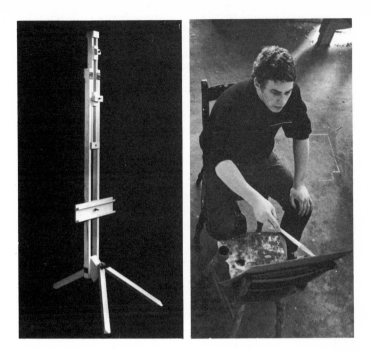

Fig. 6                 Fig. 7

There are painters who work with their painting horizontal on a table, or even the floor. Certainly, this seems a good idea if you use thin paint, unless you want your paint to run.

One can paint anywhere, in any room, but having to be careful not to spill a drop of paint can be inhibiting. Better paint in a shed or garage where you can leave your mess, rather than in a living room where every trace must be erased after a session.

# 3 The general approach

Every painting is an adventure and a journey of discovery. Each achievement reveals new problems.

This expanding, changing vision is the wonderful thing about painting. Be pleased with what you have done. But never say: 'This is it, from now on I'll stick to this way of doing it!' And when well-meaning friends try to make you repeat successful formulae — don't! (There is always somebody who will say that he liked your last painting better.)

You will never reach a stage when all is plain sailing, all problems solved. As soon as one difficulty has been mastered, further ones will appear. But, though the progress may be imperceptible, you will develop and grow, your horizons will widen.

Jump in at the deep end. Aim at complete paintings from the start. Do not put off problems of composition or background till you consider you have 'mastered the figure'. That moment will never come; the more you learn the more you see and the more there is left to learn.

At times your painting will seem to take charge. Starting your picture with a definite idea of what the finished work should look like, apparently accidental shapes and colour combinations will suggest further ones, and very soon the painting will dictate to you what to do next. Let yourself follow these impulses. They come perhaps from a part of yourself that knows best and may lead you to paint a better picture than the planned scheme.

Do not worry about lack of style in your paintings. Style is a natural growth. One's own paintings always look obvious, like one's hand writing or one's face in the mirror. So you will not even recognise it when you have achieved a style of your own.

You will inevitably be influenced by other painters. That is as it should be and it happens to all of us. It is a way of learning.

When I was at art school there was a fellow-student whose work impressed me greatly and whom I tried hard to emulate. Years later he told me that my work at art school had greatly impressed him and that he had tried hard to emulate it. I'm not sure what the moral of this is, but I think it fits in here.

Thick paint—heavy impasto—is no more artistic or stylish than thin paint. If your painting naturally builds up a heavy texture, that's fine, but don't pile it on for Art's sake. Nor is it more dashing or artistic to use a palette knife rather than a brush. Very good paintings have been done with the knife, but I am not fond of the technique. It is too easy to get a flashy, meaninglessly-textured surface and it leads to mannerisms. Think of the dreadful paintings of sailing-boats or canals in Venice one finds in furniture stores and you will know what I mean.

Paint reasonably large. It is no easier to do a small, than a large painting. The smaller the shapes you deal with, the more fussy and timid your painting is likely to become. Large is a relative term; one artist's 'large' will be another one's 'tiny'. But there is a tendency for beginners to work far smaller than they should, either from timidity or humility. If your paintings measure less than a foot in any one direction you are probably one of them.

I take for granted that you keep a sketch-book and possibly have done some life-drawing. If not, start to draw now. Get into the habit of it. Draw anything—yourself in the mirror, the cat on the mat, members of your family, inanimate objects. Draw complete things, not just details. And see them against their background; do not draw objects in isolation, put them into their setting. No object is ever seen in isolation. There is always a background. The object rests on something and is flanked and backed by other things.

Every painting starts with a linear pattern, whether it is of a still life or a nude figure. It is practice in drawing that will enable you to indicate firmly this basis of your painting. It is practice in drawing that will help you to be an artist, not knowledge of the Latin names of bones and muscles.

In the 15th century, Italian artists re-discovered the antique. They were particularly impressed by the Greek and Roman mastery of the nude human body. They attempted to reach the same standard by thorough studies in anatomy, working from cadavers and drawing and recording the muscles and bones. Renaissance artists believed that some of the ancients had known the secrets of perfect proportion and beauty, and hoped to re-discover them.

Painters and sculptors also resented being the poor relations of other disciplines, of the study of dead languages, philosphy, theology, mathematics and astronomy. By precise and academic study they hoped to raise their status from that of craftsmen.

We are now convinced that seeing freshly and personally is far more important than dry and academic knowledge. Now, even full-time art students are not taught anatomy as a separate subject. I am aware, though, how puzzling some details of the body can appear, how one feels that only a knowledge of the underlying structure could help to explain the intricacies of the surface. I hope that that these few hints may help you to cope.

There are five substances that affect the body's surface:

*Bone:* on skull, elbows, on the hip joint, collar bone, point of the shoulder, knees, shins, knuckles, ankles and under some conditions on spine and shoulder blades.

*Tendon:* showing as stringy ridges, joining muscle and bone. On neck, wrist, back of hand, heel and above the toes.

*Tensioned muscle:* gives an impression of taut firmness. Good examples are the flexed biceps or the calf muscles of someone standing on tip-toe.

*Relaxed muscle:* softer-looking, less well defined than when it is under tension.

*Fat:* mainly on buttocks, stomach, breast. The plumper the model, the greater will be the areas of fat and the deeper the layer. Men and women have the same bones and muscles. The main difference is in the greater amount of fat that overlays the muscles of women—even a thin woman will have relatively large areas of fat.

We all inhabit a body and are aware of its weight and movements. It may well be of help, when you are puzzled or worried by some uncertainty of interpretation of some aspect of the model, to be aware of that part in yourself.

Hold your hand over a white piece of paper. The hand will be a lot darker than the paper; there will be a denseness and richness of colour in it. Now place your hand against a dark background, a dark corner of the room for instance. The hand will appear luminous and you will see its *lightness*, rather than its colour. Thirdly, find a background of a similar tone to your hand and you will be aware of the light and shade on it. The modelling and solidity of your hand will be its most noticeable aspect (Fig. 8).

Against the white paper the edges of your fingers will appear

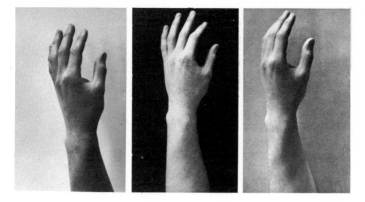

Fig. 8

so dark that black will hardly be dark enough. Yet against a dark background these same edges under the same light will become a delicate, pearly colour.

I have so far here only mentioned tone, but try similar experiments with colour. Against a bright red background your hand will look pale and grey, whereas against green it will appear rich and warm in hue.

You have posed the model and chosen the aspect and distance from which you are going to work. Now is the time to plan your composition. Try hard to imagine the finished painting on the blank board.

There is an infinite number of possibilities. The tendency of many beginners is to place the head top centre and hope for the best. But, unless the model is standing or sitting squarely and symmetrically in front of you, as in Fig. 9, it is bound to turn out badly.

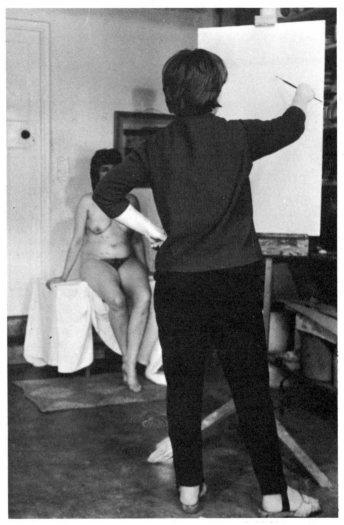

Fig. 9

Even with the figure facing you squarely, you may decide (and do decide before you start working, rather than wish you had when you have done some hours' work) not to paint the figure the obvious size—head nearly at the top, toes nearly at the bottom of the picture, Fig. 10.

Before beginning to paint, decide on your composition by means of small, diagrammatic sketches. It will save time and regrets later on. But be careful in translating your scribble into the full scale painting. When enlarging a small drawing, the essential character and boldness of the composition often get lost.

Figs. 10  11, 12, and 13

Figs. 14, 15, 16, 17

The figure need not even
be complete (Figs. 14 & 15).
But this should be intentional.
Don't just let the figure be
chopped off at the edge
by accident. Never, if your
calculations have not quite
worked out, squash the figure
into the rectangle,
shortening legs or arms, or
changing the angle of the
body just to get it all in.

There is no reason why the
figure must be the centre of
the composition. Fig. 16,
for instance, is a possibility.

Learn to see the figure
as one shape among many.
The background shapes are
equally important (Fig. 17).

28

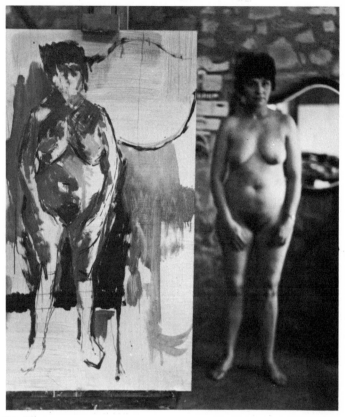

Fig. 18

To paint 'sight-size' is to make the figure on your painting the same size as the model appears from where you are. The further the model, the smaller the figure will be on the painting. If the model is six feet away from you it means a painted figure about two feet tall. A model twelve feet away will mean a painted figure about a foot high.

Painting sight-size lets you compare proportions between model and painting with some ease, but I doubt whether it should be adopted as a regular practice. The size of one's painting ought not to be arbitrarily determined by the distance one is from the model. But as one gets further away from the model there are limits to the amount of detail one sees; it is dangerous then to paint on too large a scale since, misinterpreting what one sees, one is tempted to invent detail.

Place the easel so that the model appears just to the left of the painting. Put the palette in front of, or to the right of the easel on a table or chair. You will then be able to work without unduly having to turn from model to painting and without your painting arm getting in the way. If you are lefthanded, as I am, you reverse this: the easel will be on the left and you look past it on the right.

Fig. 19

Be aware of how you hold the brush, when painting. The movement should come from the shoulder and elbow, rather than from the wrist, as in writing. Hold the brush well back along the handle. Try not to rest your hand on the painting; get used to having only the bristles in contact with the painting. A wobbly line is preferable to a cramped one (Fig. 19).

In oil painting, one colour thinly and transparently put on another is either *glazed* or *scumbled*.

*Glazing* is painting a darker colour over a light one, with the lighter colour shining through.

*Scumbling* is the opposite, a lighter colour applied transparently over a dark colour.

Glazing tends to make colours look warm and rich. Scumbling leads to cool, cloudy colour. Both are useful at times.

The origins of these techniques reach back to the 15th-century when paintings were begun in tempera and completed with thin layers of the brighter hues in oil paint. Out of this developed the theory of 'dead-colouring'. The whole painting was completed in virtual monochrome, often a dull green. Then colour was added in careful washes and stipples. Only in the latter part of the 19th century did the Impressionists finally break with this slow and over-deliberate procedure.

Linseed oil, varnish or a painting medium such as Meguilp is used to thin the pigments for glazing and scumbling. There are two reasons for this: colours thinned with turps or white spirits only are runny and difficult to control; and a very thin layer of paint without some binding medium is fragile and easily marked.

Transparent pigments are used for glazing:

Burnt Sienna, Raw Sienna, Burnt Umber, Raw Umber, Alizarin Crimson, Viridian, Prussian Blue and Ivory Black.

For scumbling the more opaque colours are used:

Yellow Ochre, Light Red, Cadmium Yellow, Cadmium Red, white and any colour mixed with white.

Sometimes the colour and tonal values of a painting go astray. It is then possible to glaze heavily large areas or even the whole painting. Once this glaze has dried you can use this dulled painting to start afresh.

I have sometimes scumbled whole skies or other large areas with white or near-white in a free and blotchy way. The results can be interesting, but this sort of thing must be approached with caution, as it so easily leads to tricks and gimmicks.

Some teachers warn against, or even try to forbid, the use of black. I think that to use black is no more wrong or dangerous than to use any other colour. No colour in itself, no hue, tint or tone, however grey or muddy, dull or sooty, can be called a bad colour. It can only look out of place in relationship to other colours which surround it or merge into it.

Certainly black ought not to be added automatically to the whole range of colours in a painting to indicate tone or shadow; but the use of any other colour in this way, for instance brown, blue or green, would be equally reprehensible.

Mix equal amounts of white with each of the colours on your palette, and observe the effect this has on the different pigments. Some colours will be affected by the white far less than others. They contain more powerful pigments and have to be used more restrainedly.

You will also find that no colour can be lightened in tone without losing brightness and changing its character. As white is added colours turn cooler. Orange becomes pink, red becomes purple-pink, browns move towards grey or mauve.

Try the same experiment, but substitute black for white, mixing half colour, half black. Again some unexpected results:

Yellow and black make a very definite green.

Black added to colours produces a range of remarkably well harmonising colours. White does the opposite: a range of colours, each mixed with white, sets my teeth on edge.

To be useful these colour tests must be done neatly, with carefully judged proportions of each pigment.

A coat of varnish on a painting will do three things:

1. It protects the surface of the painting from dirt and damage.
2. Colours will acquire an even gloss, even those that have gone matt in drying.
3. Life is added to colours; 'sunken' and dead colours regain the look they had when they were still wet.

In spite of these merits there is a strong anti-varnish movement, of which I am a member. I think that among professional painters the non-varnishers now outnumber the varnishers.

The varnishing of paintings grew from the deliberate step-by-step techniques practised by painters, who now are thought of as out of date. (I am aware of not being consistent. Glazing and scumbling too were part of these painters' practices. Yet I glaze and scumble, even if in a non-traditional way.)

Many modern painters leave large areas of canvas or board uncovered by paint. Varnish would look quite wrong on these areas. It would disguise the contrasts and qualities of paint surface—matt against glossy—which is a deliberate aspect of some non-figurative, abstract art. In my own case, the matt surface which many of my paintings have would be entirely changed by varnish.

You must decide for yourself. It is a matter of personal preference whether one varnishes one's paintings or not.

If you do varnish your paintings wait till they are absolutely dry and hard—a matter of months rather than weeks. Varnish them in a dry, warm and dust-free atmosphere, and use a soft, large brush. Be certain that the brush is not liable to lose any hair; hair embedded in varnish looks awful. Also, be methodical. The whole of the painting must receive an even coat, and it is better to give it two thin coats, than one thick one. Mastic or Copal are varnishes frequently used. But there are now Polyurethane plastic varnishes on the market which are completely clear (all traditional varnishes have a slight amber tint) and do not discolour with time.

In Hesketh Hubbard's encyclopaedia of oil painting methods, *Materia Pictoria*, there are 31 pages of information under the heading 'Varnish', so this is only a hint of the theories and arguments there are about the subject.

Fig. 20  36″ × 26″

# 4 Painting from life

**Figure 20**

Where in the discussion of a painting I write of any part of the model, *left* or *right* refer to the model's left or right arm, leg, shoulder, hip etc. Otherwise, when talking of background, composition or direction of light, for instance, left and right are referred to from your, the spectator's, point of view.

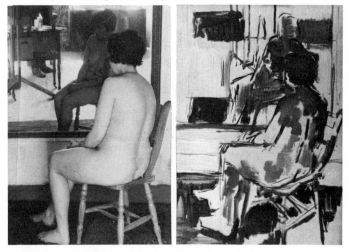

Fig. 21                    Fig. 22

This setting combines a variety of elements: chair, carpet, model, wall and mirror. In the mirror, seen against the light, are the french door, easel, table, my legs and the reflection of the model.

The photograph, Fig. 21, gives an idea of the actual appearance. The colour-plate, Fig. 20, shows the finished painting.

Distance and space can be conveyed in two ways. First, it can be stated structurally, by linear, geometric perspective with converging parellel lines and distant objects drawn smaller than near ones. Secondly, it can be implied atmospherically by means of tone and colour—aerial perspective; this is based on the fact that the further an object is away from you, the more the intervening air will change the object's colour and tone. The most obvious example are the pale, blue hills in landscapes. Turner or Seurat in their different ways were able to give very precise information about the distance of objects by this means.

In general I prefer structural solutions, but in this case, to unify the disparate parts, the second method was adopted. Mirror reflections must look like a mirror and not like a hole in the wall. This can only be done by flattening tones, by suppressing detail and modelling and by careful adjustment of colour values.

The direction of light in the mirror image is reversed. I actually had the light behind me, yet in the mirror one looks into the light. The window reflected in the mirror acts as a secondary source of light. The side of the model facing the mirror is basically in shadow, but receives some light from the mirror. This is apparent in the edges of light on shoulders, wrist and left thigh.

The pose is simple, but made difficult by the angle from which it is seen. Since it is neither back-view nor side-view, the thigh recedes towards the knee, and the left shoulder is nearer than the right. It is only too easy to try to paint both the left half in side-view and the back in back-view. I was aware of this tendency, yet I got caught painting (as shown in the detail, Fig. 23) the spine too far to the left, and giving too much prominence to the right side of the back. When I became aware of it, the whole of the back had to be re-painted and its outline restated.

Fig. 23

The key to this (and any similar pose) is an awareness of what parts of the figure are nearest to you; in other words, what parts face you. In this case it is the left shoulder, left upper arm, left flank and hip. From there all other planes recede: to the right, the plane across the shoulders, the flat, sloping slab of the shoulder-blades. The details of spine and lower back may disguise and confuse the general direction, but it is there—a recession from left to right. Receding to the left are the thigh, appearing shorter than its full length, and the very much foreshortened left arm.

After laying-in in Burnt Umber, the painting was built up in colour patches. At first I worked broadly, summarising large areas with a wide brush, gradually breaking it down, using smaller brushes, the individual touches of paint getting more delicate.

There is no contradiction in the fact that as the touches of paint become smaller, the painting becomes simpler. Textures can be complicated and subtle, yet the over-all design remain simple. On the other hand, a painting done with a six-inch brush can be a wild jumble.

The core of this composition is an arc running from the left corner of the table in the mirror, then through the easel, my legs, the reflected and actual head of the model, down her body, into the thigh and ending at the knee.

Particularly when the background is as complicated as here, one should work over the whole of the painting at the same time, not concentrating on any one bit for too long.

Individuality is the most highly prized quality in contemporary art, and teachers are reluctant to give direct and definite instruction. Every artist is expected to discover his or her own style. No generally applicable rules are accepted in painting; but this advice about working all over a painting is an exception.

Beginners do tend to proceed piece-meal, finishing one bit before going on to the next. At this stage, this is certainly not a sign of a personal style. To start with, make a great effort to deal with your painting in breadth. Then, much later, if you still feel like it, revert to completing your painting bit by bit. There are a few painters who work like this (Stanley Spencer did); they are the exception, but you may be one of them.

**Figure 28**

I decided on the setting and the lighting before posing the model. I painted by artificial light; artists often feel doubtful about this, but I see little objection. After all, paintings are seen, as often as not, in the evening.

The predominating verticals of the setting demanded a not too symmetrical pose. Thanks to a good model it took very little time to arrive at a natural, relaxed pose.

The popular idea of beauty, particularly female beauty, has degenerated from the classical antique, revived in the renaissance, through Baroque voluptuousness, Roccoco grace, arch Victorian sentimentality and insipid academicism into Hollywood and 'Girlie'-magazine, pin-up conventionality.

On the other hand there has arisen an art school convention of treating the nude: a pseudo-scientific, impersonal approach, which seems to deny the fact that you are painting a human being. Cézanne, the greatest modern master, is indirectly responsible for this. But there is always aggressive strength informing his pure and monumental figures. His works are elemental—his followers only elementary.

It is difficult to steer a course, avoiding these two ways, but it can be done. Bonnard, Modigliani, Wyndham Lewis and Francis Bacon are just four entirely different artists who have done it triumphantly.

At first the figure in Fig. 24 may seem too far to the left. But the upward slope of the legs from the left corner is balanced by a slanting line on the right, along the jar and wall into the left arm. The figure is only one element in the composition.

The drawing of the shoulders caused some difficulties and I had to check, recheck, paint and re-paint. When in doubt (as I was here) about the relationship of certain points, use a brush handle to *plumb* them. This is usually done vertically (Fig. 25) to see which points lie exactly in line above each other. It can equally well be done horizontally (Fig. 26) or at any other angle, though you must be careful to use the same angle on both model and painting. To measure relative proportions slide your thumb along the brush handle held at arm's length. The results may be surprising, particularly when you check the foreshortened parts (notice how short in this view the left forearm appears).

The light on the figure is flat and unemphatic. In spite of this the modelling can give a sense of firm solidity. A series of rounded

Fig. 24

Fig. 25          Fig. 26

shapes is important in imparting a rhythm of solid forms, such as the head, the left shoulder, the breasts, the stomach, knees and wrist. Little of the face is showing, yet the head with its lightest point at the top of the forehead keeps a spherical appearance.

We are so used to thinking of the nose as the part of the head sticking out farthest, that there is a tendency to keep it pointing forward, even if, as here, the tip of the nose is further away than the bridge.

Nowhere else in the body is so much detail concentrated in so small an area as in the head. Do not over-concentrate on it; the head should have no more importance than any other area of a similar size in the painting. Be aware of the shapes of forehead, jaw, cheeks and skull, rather than the small details of mouth, eye-brows, eyes, nostrils and ears. A head can be painted ignoring these details. Half-close your eyes and they will disappear; the eyes will get lost in the sockets, the mouth will become insignific-ant compared with the arch of the upper jaw.

The horizontal surfaces of floor, chair seat, chair arm, top of thighs, left forearm lie in parallel planes, conforming to the same perspective, sharing a common vanishing point. Try not to make chairs seems to teeter on one leg with the figure tilted above it, apparently not touching it. If you work all over, rather than paint-ing a figure and then shoving a chair under it, it will more easily come right.

I had painted in rich, contrasting colour, from warm red (top of thighs, legs) to greens and blues (chest, stomach and edge of legs). At the stage reached in Fig. 27, recession and bulk in the thighs and a sense of the change of direction at the knees was missing. In the final stages I also simplified the walls, the floor,

Fig. 27

and the chair. The hair became simpler too, to make the head more clearly spherical.

You must strive to gain in firmness and conviction, as you lose in freedom and spontaneity. Just tidying and cleaning up is no use at all, unless your forms acquire strength and your pattern clarity in the process.

It is often difficult to decide how to put on your paint; along the forms, across them, following them, horizontally or vertically. I would not try to give a general rule. Most of the time I am not aware how I do it. The actual act of painting should be largely unselfconscious. But here are a few tentative hints.

Do not draw with paint as you would with a pencil. A touch of paint has three dimensions—width and thickness as well as length.

Vary the direction of application. Good paintings have been done where every stroke runs in the same direction, but it is pretty tricky and too easily monotonous.

Often change the size of brush you use.

Vary the thickness of paint—the impasto.

Do not work more carefully along the edges of forms out of anxiety to keep a clean outline.

In the early stages of the painting I was far too concerned with trying to get the feeling of the pose and setting to bother with technical niceties. The paint got scrubbed on anyhow, as long as it went in the right place and was the right colour. Gradually the touches of paint became more precise and deliberate. Using smaller brushes, I kept the direction, size of strokes and thickness of paint varied. In the right arm, left hand and feet I followed the form. In the left leg and stomach I worked across the forms. On chest, neck and left upper arm I used vertical strokes and I put irregular touches of paint on hair and thighs.

Paint texture is very important. For instance, the right forearm and the background next to it are a similar pink-grey, yet the arm comes forward through being painted with heavier impasto and more emphatic brush-work.

Fig. 28  36″ × 26″

**Figure 31**

There are two reasons why I do not like sharply foreshortened views of the nude.

First, they are supposed to be difficult and therefore one tends to paint them in a bravura way: look how clever I am! Painting is not a circus act, and should not attempt to dazzle momentarily. Its values are more lasting.

Second, by trying to persuade the spectator that he is looking along a form into depth, the unity of the painting as a flat pattern is weakened.

But in the present case there seemed such firm structure in the design that it overcame at least the second objection. The horizontals along the left upper arm and between the thighs, the verticals of left and right lower arm, and the sloping top edge of the left thigh parallel to the right upper arm, give stability.

The painting was begun in Burnt Umber, corrected and strengthened with black. I used Prussian Blue, very diluted with white spirits, on background and hair.

The complexities of back and hip demanded some basic modelling quite early on; this was painted in blue-grey. More than an indication of photographically realistic light and shade, the modelling is meant to knit the forms together like the pieces of a jig-saw puzzle.

At the beginning I intended to paint in very cool colours and began in greys, blues and greens, making all shadows as cool as possible. Later, orange, maroon and Yellow Ochre became the predominant colours. The growth of a painting is never predictable. Even if one can't give a rational explanation for it, these departures from a pre-conceived scheme are usually based on sound intuition.

When one sees a familiar object in an unfamiliar position a conflict is set up. I *know* what a hand looks like, and yet here I am faced with something which taken in isolation does not look like a hand and would not be recognised as one. In the whole painting, apart from the right arm, there is nothing that appears in its accepted shape or at its usually accepted angle.

Many beginners try to compromise unconsciously, introducing shapes which are much nearer to what one *knows* than what one *sees*. Try to forget what you know. Try to see what is in front of you.

At times you will find it difficult to sort out the jumble of twisted

Fig. 29

shapes that make up a body. Make yourself see the figure as a single shape as though it were a pebble, a piece of wood or a stain on a wall. Later you can sub-divide and define the component parts.

As a painting progresses one often loses the force and conviction of the first few lines. Once lost, they are hard to recapture. Here, for instance, in the painting of the back, I never found again the first clarity.

The dribbly paint on head and background had to go. At times

Fig. 30

useful, here it disturbed the flat slab-like treatment of the rest. I also simplified the line along the lower edge of the figure from right elbow to the buttocks.

Dissatisfied with the background, I painted dark the whole of the area surrounding the figure, using black and Prussian Blue. Also, this allowed me to see the figure in isolation as a single shape. After the background was dry the bed was painted in warm Yellow Ochre, allowing some of the dark colour underneath to show through, giving life to the surface.

Fig. 31  33" × 26"

Colours changed, becoming warmer. The background at the top and the hair are now a deep maroon, mixed from Alizarin Crimson, Prussian Blue and Burnt Umber. The flesh is pink, orange and Light Red. Painting with broken, irregular touches, some of the original cool colour shows through, making the warm hues more positive by contrast.

With the figure painted in a flat way, a too solidly modelled head would be wrong, so the hair became a linear pattern. The direction of the strands implies the volume of the head.

**Figure 33**

The elements of this painting are seen as flat, interlocking shapes. Even the foreshortened settee, thighs and arms are seen as part of the two-dimensional pattern. The rectangular slabs of the shelves at top right are the key to the painting. There are objects of many shapes and colours on these shelves, and by half-closing my eyes they revealed their basic forms and tones. Do not be side-tracked by small, attractive details; keep your work simple. Be willing to simplify, even to suppress, in the interest of the composition. Once you have discovered scheme and order, hold on to it.

The painting was layed-in in straight lines, establishing links between figure and background: the horizontal of the lowest shelf is continued by the right thigh, the left leg continues the vertical edge of the settee-back.

The first filling in of the main areas with roughly vertical strokes of a big brush is in keeping with the flat slab-like build-up.

Cover the whole area of your paintings as soon as possible. If you leave parts unpainted for too long you get used to these blank areas. Unconsciously you adjust the painting to accommodate them, and you may find it difficult later to fill them in.

Immediately after taking the photograph for Fig. 32 I covered the whole of the painting very broadly—left wall in Burnt Sienna, floor in Raw Sienna, settee nearly black (the pattern to be painted later in lighter colours).

Before going on with the figure I worked on the background. The books became sub-divisions of the shelves, and at a later stage this pattern was echoed in the way its facets and planes sub-divide the figure. The head was treated the same way. Rather than painting eye-brows, eyes and lips, I dealt with forehead, cheeks, nose etc. in the same manner as shoulder or arms. The hair, too, was seen as part of the whole, linking with the shelf on the right and the wall on the left.

The vertical and horizontal emphasis was re-inforced; not so much in the actual direction of the brush-strokes, as for instance in the continuation of the corner of the room into the head and body. The centre of the face continues the vertical division; the right half is dark, the left half is light. Below the face the tones are reversed. A vertical line between chin and right breast divides the light right shoulder from a dark area on the chest. This sounds far too much as though it had been deliberately worked out, but

Fig. 32

a nearly accidental brush-stroke may have begun it. However, once recognised, a development of this kind should be carried through as decisively as possible.

The colours of the figure link with the background: warm pinks, greys and yellows similar to walls and floor. The pigment is put on densely and opaquely with no turps at all.

It is at least as important to keep your palette and brushes clean when working in this subdued, tonal way, as when you use strong, bright colours. Previous colour or dirty turps seeping down the ferrule of your brush will turn what was meant to be subtle colour into dirty and indeterminate colour.

Look at the changes that took place between the stage reached in Fig. 34 and the colour plate, Fig. 33, of the finished painting. The left thigh was re-painted to bring its tone closer to that of the abdomen; it had looked too detached and separate. In the left leg the vertical of the shin-bone was strengthened. Stressing the tone along the edge of the knuckles of the left hand helped to form another vertical down the right leg.

Small areas of sharper colour, pink mixed from Cadmium Red and white, contrast with the subdued and sombre colours of the skin.

A few of the books on the shelves were painted in bright pink and pure orange. My choice of colours was suggested by what was on the shelves, but I certainly did not follow slavishly what I saw. After all, the colour sequence of books on a shelf is so arbitrary that one can with the clearest conscience alter it.

In every painting you must decide afresh how much freedom to allow yourself to depart from what you actually see. Some painters find close and meticulous adherence to seen reality most rewarding. Others would find this irksome and restraining. They are only able to be true to themselves if they use what is in front of them merely as a starting-off point for their personal interpretation.

In a misguided attempt to be personal and to liven up their work, some painters will, often with the palette knife, apply a fruit salad of colours and textures. If the shapes are interesting and have meaning, there is nothing wrong with large, quite flatly-painted areas.

Particularly in the late stages of a painting, there are two very helpful things you can do:

By turning your painting upside down, you see it as an abstract arrangement and you will be able to judge its colour, design and

Fig. 33  41″ × 24″                                                    51

Fig. 34

Fig. 35 detail of Fig. 33

completeness in a fresh way. For instance, by turning *this* painting upside down I was made aware of a similarity between the angular, stepped edge of the hair against the face and the similarly serrated line along the top edge of the books. Aware of this, I was able to emphasise it.

Secondly, look at your painting in a mirror. We get so used to the painting in progress, faults and all, that only a completely new way of seeing it will make us recognise them. You may be surprised by obvious mistakes and weaknesses which you would never have noticed otherwise.

**Figure 39**

It is good general advice, I think, to ignore accidental shadows, cast shadows and highlights, and instead to translate the light and shade on the subject into an explanation of the form. There will be exceptions; in this painting, the model stood in strong cross-light and the effects of light and shade are the very theme of the painting.

This may be the place to distinguish between the various kinds of light and shade, as follows:

*Local colour:* the actual colour of any surface under a flat light (on right hip and right foot).

*Shadow:* any surface turned from the source of light (most of the back), but always affected by one of the following.

*Reflected light:* a form in shadow, but turned towards a light surface (underside of chin, back of right thigh). Reflected light can make a great deal of difference to tone and colour. Look at your hand in shadow, then bring a white piece of paper up to it and see how much lighter the colour of the skin appears; hold something brightly coloured near your hand and the hand will take on much of that colour.

*Saturated shadow:* not a generally used term, but it does describe a definite phenomenon, where two planes, both in shadow, face each other (inside of left arm and thigh). These are the deepest shadows. But be careful; they are often only very small areas. It is easy to exaggerate them and thereby to break up the continuity of form.

*Cast shadow:* the shadow of one shape falling across another, often confusing and therefore justifiably ignored (the shadow of the right forearm falling across the hip, particularly in the first stage, Fig. 36).

*Highlights:* the source of light reflected on a surface (on neck, shoulder, spine, small of back). They easily give a superficial, slick look to a painting. If you really can't do without them, put them on very restrainedly as the very last thing in the painting. I may, in fact, have rather overdone it in this painting.

Whatever the light, the actual solidity of the object or figure you paint is not affected, whether lit from left or right, top or bottom. Light can only reveal form, it does not create it.

Light and shade must be seen as colour. There is colour in shadows; in this painting, purple and warm reds on the back of the legs, greens, mauves and deep yellow on the back. Be as

Fig. 36

Fig. 37

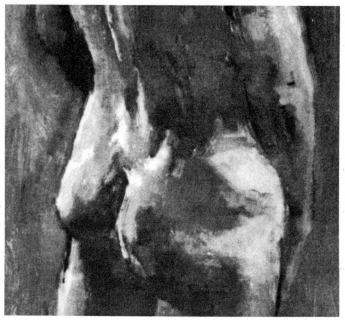

Fig. 38 detail of Fig. 39

daring as possible; never just add black or brown to the skin colour.

Colour, once put on your painting, cannot be deepened or lightened by adding another colour to it. Either let the original colour dry before re-painting, or scrape it off with a palette-knife. Be ruthless. A scraped area has its own character and will often in itself suggest a solution.

The head and neck, being badly placed, were scraped off in this painting after stage two, Fig. 37. In the finished head there are appreciable patches of scraped board visible. This does not show in the reproduction, but in the original it plays a positive part.

Drastic alterations are possible, but there are times when one has to decide whether to discard a painting and to start again. But discarding can be over-indulged in. It may prove one's artistic temperament to fling half-done paintings on the fire, but only the artist's colour-men profit from this. You will learn more by carrying on as far as is humanly possible and *then* starting again. The nearly abandoned painting may even turn out to be a good one. The struggle you had in coming to terms with the problem can add strength and conviction to the painting; an easily painted picture is not always the best.

The exact line followed by the edge of a shadow is important in demonstrating the solidity of a form. Abrupt change from light to dark (as on the spine) indicates sharp changes of planes. Gradual change from light to dark (as on hip or thigh) means a round, fleshy form (Fig. 38). Every shadow edge is a potential contour and a precise indication of solidity. (It is by the analysis of shadow edges that moon maps are drawn from photographs sent back from space satellites.)

Any one of three different aspects can be the strongest in a painting: modelling, light and shade, or colour. In modelling one conveys solidity by tonal graduation. Light and shade make for a pattern of dark and light. Colour can give a sense of solidity and a feeling of light. You will gradually discover in which direction your own taste and talent lie.

My own paintings stress modelling at the expense of the other two. I am interested primarily in the solidity of objects. The fact that I am a sculptor, as well as a painter, probably explains this.

From Giotto to Cézanne there were painters to whom modelling and solid reality were of first importance; Caravaggio, La Tour and Rembrandt were fascinated by the play of light and shade; Matisse, Van Gogh or Kokoschka interpreted largely in colour.

Working on this painting I became too interested in individual shapes. In Fig. 37 you can see how the painting was becoming a number of unconnected parts. One half of the back is painted without regard for the other; the planes of the right arm are not linked to the shoulder; the legs and thighs are not seen as a pair. But the basic drawing and stance of the figure was reasonably firm and I could unify it within that framework.

In a standing figure the distribution of weight between the two feet must be conveyed or the figure is in danger of seeming to float insubstantially. The stance literally hinges on the pelvis. Back and thighs are anchored there. See how far the shoulders are set back, the angle of the back sloping into the hips and how far the hips themselves are in front of the feet. Plumbing can help to check on the relative positions, but don't rely on it too much; good painting comes from observation, not from measuring.

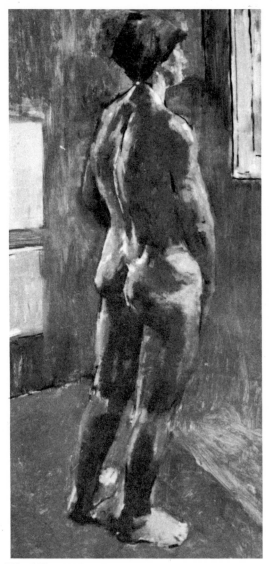

Fig. 39  36" × 16"

**Figure 42**

I used to like rather complex poses, but now they seem contrived and obtrusive. I feel that simple ones, like this, give more scope.

I painted sitting down, because from a low view-point, back, shoulders and head made an interesting continuous shape. But sitting down is not to be recommended on a painting this size. You are cramped, too near the painting and probably will not get up often enough to step back to see it as a whole.

Quite early on the tone on thigh, back, head and stomach was put in to make the light shapes on arm, shoulder and hip into positive areas.

All the significant modelling in this painting is within a very narrow band along the outline of the figure. The curving away of the stomach had to be conveyed on the strip between the arm and the outline of the body. The left shoulder-blade is much further away than the right and yet they appear close together. Across the hips and the small of the back complex planes are condensed into the width of a brush-line.

The least movement by the model, or the painter, could significantly change the contour.

The outline is always the furthest visible point of any solid shape. Yet the edge, which therefore you have to paint as turning away and receding, is the clearest indication of form.

After the areas of dark tone have been indicated, the light areas must have colour applied to them. Otherwise there is a danger of unconsciously regarding the white painting ground as the right tone for the light areas, and the colours used for the darker tones will be keyed and adjusted to white. When finally you paint the light areas you may

Fig. 41

well find that all the heavier tones must be strengthened to retain the right relationship.

As the lines of back, arms and front of body are so nearly parallel and yet subtly and significantly varied, so the planes that face you are simple and unemphatic: forward from the shoulder through shoulder-blade and arm, then inwards into the waist, out again from waist into hip, then in down the thigh. Along these planes there may be small dents and lumps. Don't make too much of them. If you were to face the model's back, what is outline now would become part of the planes facing you. The outline then would run across parts which face you now. Outline and interior modelling are inextricably connected; are in fact, one and the same thing. Between simple outlines there is bound to be simple modelling.

I had intended to keep the background about the same tone as the darker parts of the figure, making shoulder and hip stand out as positive light areas. The light parts stood out, but the rest of the figure merged into the background. In particular, the legs looked insubstantial (Fig. 41).

By lightening the background something was lost; the light part of the figure lacks luminosity and stands out less well. But more was gained. She stands more firmly and the forward movement has more life. The colours of the skin, in spite of their paleness, appear more positive. There is more air and space around the figure. The shapes of the background play a more positive part.

Small and quite unimportant light or dark areas, such as the dent in the elbow, easily get exaggerated. This over-emphasis on small detail is a common fault. Being surrounded by a light area a small dark spot will look darker than it really is. The same goes, of course, for light detail against a dark background.

Do not grudge time spent in analysing, rather than actual painting. Frequently look at your painting from a distance, comparing it with the model. Look at the painting in a mirror. Turn it upside-down. Be self-critical; it will make you a better painter.

Fig. 42  36″ × 19″

**Figure 44**

The more accidental effects of light and shade ought probably not to be imitated by the painter; they belong rather to the photographer and movie maker. The painter's aim should be to discover structure and to base his work on the essential form of what he is painting: not unlike the sculptor, who only wants his model lit in such a way that he can most clearly see the changes of form and surface.

Modelling and solidity can only be conveyed by the means available to the painter: colour, tone and the direction of his brush strokes. This directional emphasis of your brush strokes can play an important part in showing solidity. No good painting has ever been produced by copying unthinkingly—whether from a photograph or from nature.

Painting this strictly symmetrical pose, I gave some importance to the pattern of light and shade. Thus, the light, apart from helping to explain the form, creates the diagonal from the right breast, across the body to the left hand.

When, as in this painting, the arms cut across a shape—between waist and hip—you must ensure that the shape *does* continue behind the arms. It is so easy to paint down to the arms and then down from the arms, ignoring that the form behind the arms is continuous. If you are at all unsure of a partly obscured shape, ask the model to move the obscuring arm—or it may be leg or head—to let you see the form clearly and uninterrupted.

Details of face and hands were softened and flattened so as not to distract from the basic shapes. The figure is widest and most boldly modelled around the middle. Towards the head and towards the feet, it narrows and the shapes get thinner. When such a pattern reveals itself to you, make sure that you also convey it to the spectator. You may have to subordinate interesting detail. This hurts, but it is worth it, if it allows the more important areas to play their full part.

The amount of detail in the relatively small areas of face, hands and feet compared with the rest of the body gives them undue prominence. Presumptuously, I may seem to criticise nature for putting fine detail at the ends—above the neck, below the wrist and ankles. But our primary concern is not with natural appearances; it is with personal observation, with picture-making. Whatever your subject-matter, it is the final painting that matters and how well it works as an expression of your ideas and personality.

Fig. 43

I had intended an entirely plain background, but when the model by chance stood in front of the mirror I recognised an affinity between their shapes: shoulders and arms echoed by the curves of the mirror.

As the painting proceeded, the drawing was refined in black with a fine sable brush. These lines were left showing in the final painting. This business of drawn outlines on paintings is an odd one. We see the edge of an object by tone, colour and stereoscopic three-dimensional vision. But drawing—representing solids by means of lines on a flat surface—has been the first, instinctive means ever since a caveman scratched the outlines of a mammoth on a piece of bone. We recognise an artist's strength by his line. In many of Van Gogh's paintings, for instance, the direction of brush strokes, not only on the edges of forms, but right across them, is what gives them urgency and fire.

In any case, every brush stroke, however delicately applied, however close in tone to the one next to it, has direction. Unless you use sprayed paint or coloured paper, paintings will be constructed of brush *lines*.

But remember, a linear technique can become self-consciously mannered with a lot of writhing lines that have no real meaning. Secondly, one way of painting should be used consistently throughout. If you establish a rich, linear texture in one part of your painting, it must be related to every other part in technique. Some painters, Francis Bacon for instance, paint the figure in a style quite divorced from the way the background is painted. But he is an exceptional artist, who has developed a style over years and is aware of what he is doing.

Fig. 44  36″ × 22″

# 5 Painting from drawings

'Squaring up' makes quite certain that you retain the exact proportions of a drawing in the painting.

Draw diagonals across your drawing, then horizontal and vertical lines through the centre where the two diagonals meet. Continue subdividing with diagonals, horizontals and verticals. Any area without detail can be ignored; others of intricate detail can be further dissected (Fig. 45).

To keep the drawing unmarked, you can pin or Sellotape (Scotch tape) tracing paper over it and draw the network on that.

Place the drawing in a corner of a piece of primed hardboard and carefully draw the continuation of one diagonal in charcoal across the board (Fig. 46). The painting, whatever its size, will be the same proportion as the drawing, as height will remain in the same ratio to width. In this case a 7 in. × 9 in. drawing was enlarged to a 21 in. × 27 in. painting.

Fig. 45

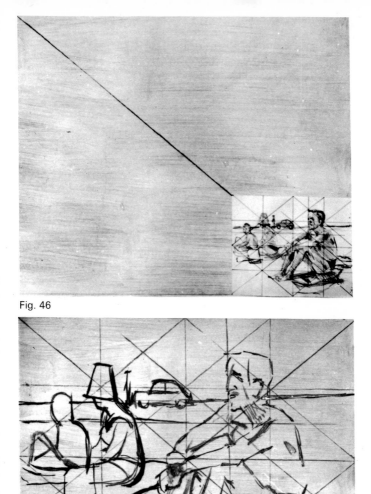

Fig. 46

Fig. 47

Fig. 48  21" × 27"

Now draw in charcoal the same network on your piece of hardboard. Then, using your diagonals etc. as a guide, transfer the lines of the drawing. Some painters use Indian ink and a pen for this. I use oil paint and a fine brush (Fig. 47). Be sure that the lines you draw on the panel cross the network in the same relative positions as in the drawing.

An alternative method is literally to 'square up'—to divide the drawing into squares and to draw an equivalent network of squares on the painting ground. The number of squares horizontally and vertically must of course agree on both drawing and painting.

If your painting is very large, a mural for instance, this is the usual method, as the drawing of diagonals along a ruler would be impossible.

I would advise you to use the diagonal method where possible, for this reason: the compositional structure of many paintings is based on diagonals. The diagonals you draw may clarify this.

When the drawing is transferred, dust the charcoal off with a rag (it leaves hardly a trace). Sickert used to leave the lattice of the squaring up showing on the finished painting; an affectation

Fig. 49

which has little justification beyond showing that the painting was done from a drawing.

The character of the drawing must influence the painting, however well you remember the original subject. To some degree the drawing becomes the subject of the painting and not just a reminder of what you saw.

Working from a strongly shaded drawing, I at first followed the tonal scheme closely in the painting (Fig. 48).

I used no black. The darkest colours—hair and bathing costume—are Prussian Blue mixed with Raw Umber. The man's body in the shadow is green-khaki, the shadows on the towel are deep blue. The towels in sunlight are the same colour as the sky (light blue), the sand is pale yellow-green. Only in the group on the left is there warm colour (pink on figures and beach-bag).

Towards the end I flattened and simplified the figures considerably. The silhouettes of the main shapes were more important than the detail within them; the dark bathing costumes and the shadows on the ground echo each other; the light shapes of beach-bag, straw hat and car window tie up.

The broken paint which made up the figures in the earlier stages has not been entirely lost in the re-painting, adding variety and contributing to the solidity.

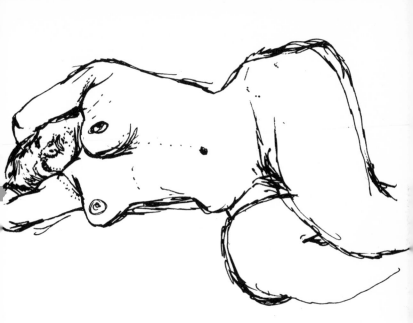

Fig. 50

## Figure 51

This drawing was one of several drawn from the model at one session. At the time I had no thought of using them for paintings. Years later I came across them in a sketch-book and decided to use this one as the foundation of a painting.

I was struck by the shape made by the background in the left bottom corner and the rather landscape-like silhouette at the top, with its varying slopes along arm, torso, hip and the vertical descent along the left thigh.

To give the maximum effect to the inter-linking of the shapes, to let the background shapes be read positively, I have treated the figure very simply. It is painted in a nearly flat pale grey with only a little warm tone here and there. The bed is virtually white. The wall is black, the pattern on it is orange and grey. The pattern invented for this has a vertical emphasis to counteract the strongly horizontal main shapes of the painting.

Apart from this pattern, the only thing not in the drawing, the only part invented in the basic composition, is the line dividing bed from wall. This was put at the level it is to give the maximum chance to the two background shapes—the white bed and the black wall. If this horizontal division were any lower, the hair would have confused it. If it were any higher, neither the curve of left forearm and elbow nor the curve of the hip would make its full impact and the black shape of the wall would have been blunter and weaker.

The drawing was done in minutes, and the head was drawn without turning the paper. As nearly always happens when drawing a familiar object at an unfamiliar angle, it became distorted.

It is extraordinary how difficult it is to draw exactly what one sees without being able to call on preconceived notions and too much familiarity with the object. How hard one has to look and how carefully to observe, if one is to escape the expected and the commonplace solution.

I accepted the distorted head as fitting well within the arms and breast, not giving too much prominence to the head's volume and separateness, and I tried to utilise this in the painting.

The edge of the figure follows a complicated series of forms. From bottom right moving anti-clockwise, the edge of the right leg leads into the sphere of the knee, upwards along the round thigh into the drooped stomach; horizontally along the ribcase, the right breast and arm; then round the elbow, upwards along the sharply receding right forearm to the hair. A similar sequence is repeated along the top from the left forearm to the left hip, and then forwards and downwards along the model's left thigh. In spite of this complexity, for the sake of the flat pattern I have used the minimum of three-dimensional emphasis. The painting of the figure is flat with just a flicker of tone and colour change rather than solid modelling.

As often with my work, this painting underwent many drastic and fundamental changes before reaching the final shape. If my description gives an impression of a deliberate and planned sequence, this is only because it would have been impossible to follow all dead ends, false starts and second and third thoughts. But the final form must have been lurking at the back of my mind.

It was painted over a period of weeks, sometimes only for a half-hour at a time. So the actual painting time would be quite impossible to estimate—even if it were of importance. For it is neither virtuous to spend ages on a painting nor is it a sign of genius to do it in 20 minutes.

Fig. 51  24″ × 32″

Fig. 52

**Figure 57**

This sketchbook drawing, on which the painting, Fig. 57, is based, was done several years ago. When I came to paint it, I had forgotten details of colour, modelling of background, but I could well remember that the sofa had slim, straight legs.

Fig. 53

In this scribble, which I did as a preliminary for the painting, I made the contrast between the solid, compact top-half and the in-substantial legs of the sofa the main compositional interest.

If you go to the trouble of doing a preliminary drawing to arrive at a satisfactory composition, do follow it as closely as you can in your painting. It is an excellent idea to square it up to retain the vital essence of its composition.

I blocked in the painting with Burnt Umber and a fairly large hog-hair brush, trying to retain some of the freedom and simplicity of the first design. From the first I had intended the sofa to be the strongest, most positive, dark shape, so that was filled in with thinned black paint very early on.

As the figure slopes up from right to left, the sofa and the edge of the floor counterbalance this by sloping slightly the opposite way, up from left to right.

The eye, placed too far back in the head, and the not too well-drawn left arm caused trouble later. Take this as a warning. A painting must be 'right' at any stage. Nothing that is fundamentally wrong will improve simply by being painted over more elaborately.

By the time the whole board is covered in paint (Fig. 55) the ultimate colour scheme and tonal relationships should be stated. You may, of course, decide to change it quite drastically later, but to see what one had intended originally is a prerequisite.

Some painters do what is, in effect, a wash drawing with heavily thinned paint before covering it in opaque paint. This appears to me an unnecessary step. The painting, done in delicate washes may look charming, but does not indicate with any force or clarity the finally intended effect. If you follow your wash indications too closely, the finished painting will either be timid and lack strength, or you must, to all intents and purposes, start again when you begin to use opaque paint.

I realise that this advice goes against widely established practice, but I can only advise what I myself have found practical and of use. I do not use very thick paint, but I do, almost from the start, mix white into my colours, rather than letting the white ground play any part.

My palette for this painting was: *white, Yellow Ochre,* Raw Sienna, *Burnt Sienna,* Raw Umber, Viridian, *Prussian Blue* and *black.* The same painting could have been painted with the colours printed in *italics* only.

Background and figure were laid in with a decorator's 1 in. brush, the wall a purple-pink, the floor a warm brown-pink. Quite deliberately I use a coarse, even clumsy, technique at this early stage. If this early paint is put on too handsomely you may well find yourself reluctant to change it at a later stage. By working coarsely at first you force yourself to refine and reconsider what you have done. But, paradoxically, you may be surprised how much of your first paint-layer shows on the finished work; proving that the less one is concerned with finish and the less self-

Fig. 54

consciously one works, the better one is likely to paint.

Working from a black and white drawing you are not helped —
or hindered — by colour confronting you. Unless at the time of
doing your drawing you made most elaborate, written colour
notes, you must invent colour. You can be as adventurous and
unrealistic as you like.

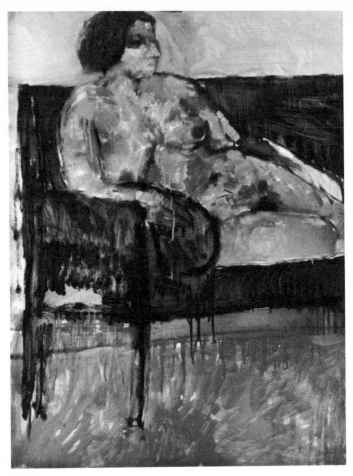

Fig. 55

Fig. 56

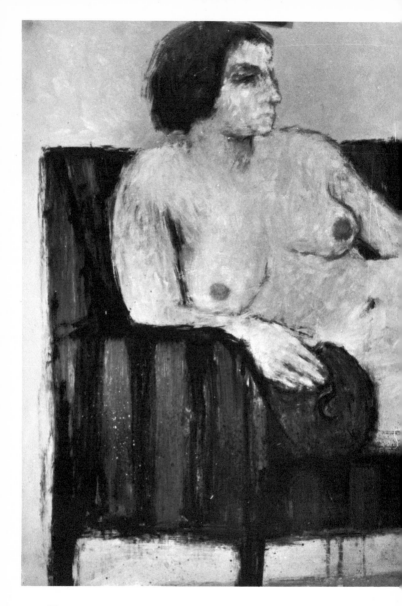

When painting anything from nature (it need not be a life paint-ing; the same applies to any subject, landscape or still-life) one is constantly overawed by the subtleties of reality. The inevitable changes of light, the slightest movement of one's model, can entirely change the character of what is in front of one. We despair of ever capturing the real essence.

Working from a drawing one does not feel this intimidating effect. But the degree of distortion in the colour should be on a par with the drawing—a realistic drawing demands realistically feasible colour. The more stylised the drawing, the freer the colour can become. All elements of a work of art must be in harmony with each other.

For instance, in Picasso's Blue Period paintings the colour is only very slightly less realistic than the drawing, yet how man-nered this makes these paintings look. (I do not denigrate Picasso, these paintings are masterpieces, but mannered masterpieces.)

To return: vertical stripes were added to the sofa, because the painting needed some vertical emphasis. The sofa legs had looked too isolated; now they logically follow the stripes downwards.

There were several things which did not satisfy me. The head had to be re-painted, moving the eye forward; I also re-painted the left arm. The right forearm and hand had to be placed firmly behind the arm rest—it had looked like a thin, weak arm resting on top of it. By simplifying the tones of thighs and abdomen I gave a sense of weight and volume to the lower part of the figure, balancing and supporting the broad upper part.

I had set out with a far bolder painting in mind than the one that finally emerged. So I started another version, the same size, trying to adhere more closely to my original intentions (Fig. 58). I arranged the tonal scheme so that the figure and the sofa made one block.

In the finished, but still very free, painting, the component parts interlock more firmly. The colours, Yellow Ochre, light red and black, contribute to the ruggedness (Fig. 59).

Whether the second painting is better than the first, even whether I like it better, I find difficult to decide. The fact that it is closer to my original intention gives me some satisfaction, and to be able to compare two versions of one subject is always instructive.

Fig. 57 detail of complete painting, 36" × 24"

Fig. 58

Fig. 59  36″ × 24″

Fig. 60

A spontaneous sketch-book drawing of someone sitting quite naturally on the beach can be a better basis for a painting than a carefully posed model in the studio.

Fig. 61   48″ × 34″

The strong pattern made by shadow on the upper part of the figure is contrasted with the lower half. Here colour replaces light and shade; and pink legs, black bathing costume and white towel on the orange sand give the feeling of bright sunlight. This scheme was of course suggested by the uncompleted modelling of the drawing.

**Figure 63**

Fig. 62

Fig. 63  38" × 48"

Holidaymakers on a beach are a fine subject for the figure painter. It is the one place in everyday life where the near-naked body is seen as a matter of course. Their relaxed, natural poses and the compact groups into which they accidentally arrange themselves have served many painters well. Sunbathers keep still long enough for one to do reasonably informative drawings. The seaside is the place where people seem to take least notice of an artist with a sketch-book. So if you are a bashful sketcher, the seaside is the place for you.

These two sketch-book pages (Fig. 62) and the painting done from one of them have a considerable degree of distortion — greater, I think, than one would advocate or usefully discuss in a book of this kind. But I thought you might be interested in seeing where my own interest in the figure has led me.

The colours of the painting — white sea, mauve sand, yellow and brown figures — are a long way from photographic realism, but give a feeling of stifling heat and blinding sunlight.

Fig. 64

This sketch-book drawing was the basis for the painting (Fig. 65); a drawing which I hardly considered worth keeping when I did it. But its very awkwardness made it possible to take liberties with it, which a better drawing would have inhibited.

The curly, convoluted pattern forming the background at the top of the painting relates to the way the figure is seen. The arms and the way they come twisting out of the shoulders, the lines from the arm-pits around the breasts, the wavy fold across the

Fig. 65  40" × 36"

stomach, the jig-saw-puzzle-like shapes of legs and feet—all this is based on what appears clumsy in the drawing.

The painting is in near monochrome; basically the only colours used were Burnt Umber, black and white. The flatness of the lower background denies any illusion of a receding plain on which the figure sits. It is a dusty pinkish-brown (Burnt Umber and white). Against cooler shades of brown and grey this seems a positive and rich colour.

# 6 Painting from photographs

You may be tempted to work from photographs. There is none of the trouble and expense of getting models. The camera solves every problem of perspective and foreshortening.

But photography is not an easy way out. Photographs are not a ready-made two-dimensional equivalent of living reality. The painter must use the intrinsic qualities of the photograph itself as his raw material.

There is today an upsurge of interest in photography by painters; many are particularly influenced by blurred news photographs and the grainy texture of the coarse half-tone dot. Francis Bacon, for instance, has found inspiration in film stills and early photographic records of human and animal movement.

Fig. 66

I took this photograph on a Spanish beach. In the painting (Fig. 67), I exaggerated the obscurities of the tangle of arms and legs and the vagueness of the two lower figures on the right.

The figures are painted without attempt at modelling, other than that suggested by the photoprint. It would be wrong to try to reconstruct, to 'improve' on your source.

Fig. 67  40" × 48"

Working from a black and white photograph the colours had to be invented. They are very simple—bright blue sky, darker grey-blue sea, white sand, grey and reddish-brown figures.

There are vast numbers of photographs of nudes in 'Health and Beauty' and 'Girlie' magazines. They can only be used for paintings with tongue in cheek, satirical intention, as the Pop painters do. On the whole, these coyly posed, too-well-lighted and conventionally composed photos are of no use to the painter.

# 7 Copying paintings

A reproduction of *Eve* by
Lucas Cranach, dated 1528,
had been hanging in my studio
for some months. At first
sight a frivolous renaissance
pin-up, painted with little
knowledge or regard for
anatomy, it is in fact a subtly
and firmly constructed design.

A bold curve runs from the
head down her left arm, across
to the right hip, into the
right leg and forward to come
to a stop in the left foot.
There is a complex series of
echoes and elaborations of
these curves. The head, the
hands, the feet, are small-scale
variations on this theme. A
line from the right shoulder
down along breast and body
has a subtly varied echo on
the right: from arm-pit to waist
and hip.

One only becomes fully
aware of a painting's subtleties
when one attempts to copy it.

I think it is nearly useless
to copy drawings or paintings
from instructional books
done by competent, but
certainly not great, artists. It is
unlikely to teach you to draw
or paint realistically. Only
working from the model can
do that. The point of copying
is to discover something
about art itself, about composition, style and formal

Fig. 68

94

discoveries made by masters. Even a quick pencil diagram will show an artist's intention more clearly than a long period of just looking at the painting.

Copying the Cranach, I deliberately painted the figure against a light background rather than the black one of the original. I had recently completed the painting reproduced in Fig. 42 and felt that there were some similarities of shape between it and this painting. By putting Cranach's Eve against a light background, I hoped to learn something about my painting.

But it is a good idea, in any case, deliberately to alter some such aspect of the painting you copy. This will force you to think about what you are doing more than if you were automatically to follow the original in all its aspects.

By painting a light background, I was also able to develop the modelling of the figure itself more clearly than a dark background would have permitted.

Fig. 69 35″ × 12″

# 8 Other approaches

Jack Yates says about this painting:

'Done in oils on hardboard, it is one of a set of 3 paintings of nudes in a tiled bathroom. All three narrow, upright, about two-thirds white wall, one third dark tiled floor, light bulb high up . . .

The painting done in one afternoon – 3 to 4 hours . . .

Adapted from a number of drawings done from the model in a bathroom . . .

Tension between figure and light bulb . . .

Nude in extreme left-hand bottom corner; her eyes and direction of glance bring her into the picture, link her to the rest. This is most important; were her eyes to look to left or forward out of the painting, it would not hold together . . .!

To explore any subject by painting a series on the theme is a splendid device for developing one's potentials to the full. It is the best way of moulding a personal style.

In this particular painting, quite a small one, the figure is composed of rounded, compact shapes. Head and neck, breasts, arm, thighs, all are simple solids; the right hand is not even allowed to interrupt the line of left hip and thigh.

Dark hair against light wall, light flesh against dark floor, give the figure importance quite out of proportion to the small area she takes up.

Movement contributes too, spiralling upwards from the bottom edge. The right thigh, the arm, the line from left hip across the body into chin and right cheek thrusts the figure like a screw into the picture space. Even the horizontal line between floor and wall bends, is seemingly pushed upwards by the growth of the figure. (Look at the painting upside down and you will be able to appreciate this even more clearly.)

This painting shows well the scope of feeling and expression that figure painting can contain.

Fig. 70 25" × 11", oil on hardboard, by Jack Yates

Fig. 71 24" × 22", gouache on cartridge paper, by June Jackson

Two gouache paintings by June Jackson on white drawing paper. Gouache is simply a high class name for poster colour or body colour. It is opaque, quick drying and the only medium needed is water. Hog hair or watercolour brushes can be used.

Mrs. Jackson has this to say about her paintings:
'Only red and Raw Umber were used in this painting, painted in about one hour. Large unpainted areas form positive shapes, indicating different distances, but no part can be nominated 'background'. Space and structure are more important than factual information (red drapes, brown chair . . .).

Fig. 72 36" × 22", gouache on cartridge paper, by June Jackson

'The figure in this painting (done in about 6 hours) is part of a complex of shapes with boldly patterned draperies. The bright fabrics force a close scrutiny of colour relationships and the interaction of the colours of setting and figure . . . Any colour is affected by surrounding colours.'

Fig. 73 20" × 30", by John Nicoll

John Nicoll began this painting working from the model. Later he returned to the painting, simplifying the tones and strengthening the contours. Most of this is done with the palette knife. With very simple means—nearly entirely in two tones—he has conveyed not only solidity, but also a feeling of space. I may have dismissed work with the palette knife as prone to textural trickery, but here the broken paint texture it produces has not been used for its own sake. By skilful variation of its density it tells you a great deal about the relative softness and hardness of forms and their position in space.

# 9 Other techniques

There has been, with the exception of June Jackson's paintings, Figs. 71 and 72, little reference to techniques other than oil paint in this book so far. Do not think that therefore it is the only worthwhile medium.

Gouache, watercolour, distemper, emulsion paints, acrylic colours are all worth trying. Mixed techniques, using coloured inks, crayons and pastels give interesting results.

Even if ultimately you decide that oil paint suits you best, it will not have been a waste of time having experimented with other media. When you return to oils you will find that it has improved your technique, that new effects and textures suggest themselves.

There is no hard division between drawing and painting. Pen or chalk drawings can have wash added. They can be elaborated with coloured crayons and emphasised or corrected with body colour. Charcoal can be used boldly for large drawings; the stick of charcoal used sideways equates a broad brush. Black or red Conté crayon has a velvety richness that rivals painting.

Very beautiful and delicate effects can be achieved with pastels. Unfortunately they have been used by some really bad painters for cheap and sentimental portraits and therefore have fallen into disrepute. But splendid and exciting work has been done with them, by Toulouse-Lautrec, Degas and Vuillard for instance.

When you use any of these techniques, begin as you intend to continue. Wash drawings are best done with a brush right from the start. Use pale washes first; any mistakes you make can later be corrected with bolder tones and will then be quite unnoticeable. Pen drawings are lifeless if they are traced over preliminary pencil lines; start with the pen.

Do not think of these techniques as cheap or inferior substitutes for oils. They exist in their own right.

# 10 Further study

No one lives in an aesthetic vacuum; our work is influenced by other artists and by what has gone before.

Reproductions and illustrations in books are only poor second-bests, but they give a hint of the artist's intentions.

Here are a number of painters, closely concerned with the human figure, the study of whose work can profit you. Books have been published on every one of them, but details of publishers and prices would be out of date by the time this appears in print.

| | |
|---|---|
| Francis Bacon | Gustav Klimt |
| Pierre Bonnard | Oskar Kokoschka |
| Paul Cézanne | Amadeo Modigliani |
| Gustave Courbet | Pablo Picasso |
| Edouard Degas | Auguste Renoir |
| Richard Diebenkorn | Egon Schiele |
| Paul Gauguin | Henri de Toulouse-Lautrec |
| Karl Hofer | |

To learn something about the historical background and the implications of the subject you cannot do better than to read Sir Kenneth Clark's *The Nude;* it is available as a paperback.

If you are curious about the theories, techniques and traditional materials of oil painting, Hesketh Hubbard's *Materia Pictoria* is a mine of information.

Finally, if I have not persuaded you that the theoretical study of anatomy is an overrated aid to figure painting, there are a great number of books on the subject. Thomson's *Anatomy for Artists,* one of the older ones, is a sound, sensible one.

Look at as much good original work as you can; go to museums and exhibitions. The more good painting you see, the more you become aware of what painting can mean, the better a painter you are likely to become. The nearer our own time the paintings are, the more immediately they speak to us. To dismiss paintings as leg-pulls is too easy. No artist works year after year, tongue-in-cheek, trying to fool us. If today an artist's work puzzles you, give it a chance; in a year's time it may have meaning for you. Keep looking with an open mind.

# For further reading

Painting the human figure by Moses Soyer, edited by R W Gill. Studio Vista, London, 1967. Watson-Guptill, New York, 1964.

Painting the nude by Jan De Ruth. Watson-Guptill, New York, 1967.

Drawing lessons from the great masters by Robert Beverly Hale. Studio Vista, London, 1965. Watson-Guptill, New York, 1964.

Dynamic anatomy by Burne Hogarth. Watson-Guptill, New York, 1965.

On the art of drawing by Robert Fawcett. Studio Vista, London, 1958. Watson-Guptill, New York, 1958.

Bridgman's complete guide to drawing from life. Foulsham, London, 1952. Sterling, New York, 1952.

# Acknowledgments

For kind permission to reproduce paintings thanks are due to
The William Ware Gallery, Fig. 70
Mrs. June Jackson, Figs. 71 and 72
John Nicoll esq., Fig. 73
I wish to thank Messrs. Winsor & Newton Ltd. for the photograph, Fig. 6, and in particular for providing the artists' materials used for Figs. 2, 3, 4 and 5.

# Index